YOU TABBIE

LIVRO DO ALUNO

1

ADRIANA SAPORITO • SUELI VALENTE

© Adriana Beatriz Saporito e Sueli Valente da Silva Caparroz, 2014

Diretora editorial: Ana Claudia Ferrari
Gerente editorial: Gisele Aga
Coordenadora de produto: Carla Rodrigues Riquena
Editora de arte: Simone Oliveira Vieira
Designer: Ivan Toledo Prado
Assistente de arte: Carol Duran
Assistente de redação: Elena Regina Pucinelli
Coordenador de produção gráfica: Márcio Borges
Assistentes de produção gráfica: Denise Taioqui e Liliam Costa

Editora de projeto: Gisele Aga
Editoras de conteúdo: Bruna Marini e Gisele Aga
Editoras-assistentes: Gabriela Farcetta e Vivian Viccino
Assistentes editoriais: Andréa Medeiros, Carla Maurício Vianna, Duda Albuquerque (Folia de Letras) e Renata Chimim
Preparadora: Maria Estela Alcântara
Revisores técnicos: Thelma de Carvalho Guimarães e Vinicius Oliveira de Macedo
Revisor linguístico: Robert Caudle Garner
Manual do professor (introdução): Juliana Tavares e Louise Potter
Letras e músicas: Cláudia Mol e Kênia Chantal (Blue Bell Ensino de Idiomas)
Projeto gráfico e edição de arte: Simone Oliveira Vieira
Diagramação: Carol Duran, Denise Martins, Ivan Toledo Prado e Tatiane Santos
Ilustrações: Alberto Stefano, Camila de Godoy, Dam Ferreira e Mauro Souza
Iconografia: Sílvia Nastari (Toca da Imagem)
Tratamento de imagens: Paulo César Salgado
Capa: Gus Morais

Livro digital interativo
Coordenação de projeto: Carina Guiname Shiroma e Vicente Martínez
Estúdio digital: Editora Globaltec
Estúdio de áudio: Núcleo Serviços Audiovisuais

```
Dados Internacionais de Catalogação na Publicação (CIP)
      (Câmara Brasileira do Livro, SP, Brasil)

     Saporito, Adriana Beatriz
        You tabbie / Adriana Beatriz Saporito, Sueli
     Valente da Silva Caparroz. -- Cotia, SP :
     Macmillan, 2014.

        ISBN 978-85-7418-940-6 (v. 1, student's book)
        ISBN 978-85-7418-945-1 (v. 1, teacher's book)
        ISBN 978-85-7418-941-3 (v. 2, student's book)
        ISBN 978-85-7418-946-8 (v. 2, teacher's book)
        ISBN 978-85-7418-942-0 (v. 3, student's book)
        ISBN 978-85-7418-947-5 (v. 3, teacher's book)
        ISBN 978-85-7418-943-7 (v. 4, student's book)
        ISBN 978-85-7418-948-2 (v. 4, teacher's book)
        ISBN 978-85-7418-944-4 (v. 5, student's book)
        ISBN 978-85-7418-949-9 (v. 5, teacher's book)

        1. Inglês (Ensino fundamental) I. Caparroz,
     Sueli Valente da Silva. II. Título.

14-01891                                    CDD-372.652

           Índices para catálogo sistemático:

        1. Inglês : Ensino fundamental    372.652
```

Reprodução proibida. Art. 184 do Código Penal e Lei 9.610 de 19 de fevereiro de 1998.
Todos os direitos reservados.
Impresso no Brasil

MACMILLAN EDUCATION
Av. Brigadeiro Faria Lima, 1.309 - 3° Andar - Jd. Paulistano
São Paulo - SP - 01452-002
www.macmillan.com.br
Atendimento ao professor: (11) 4613-2278
0800 16 88 77 (Outras regiões)
Fax: (11) 4613-2237

Créditos das fotos:

Capa: Tru9ja/Dreamstime.com

p. 7: Pavel Losevsky/iStock/Thinkstock; Jupiterimages/Goodshoot/Thinkstock; p. 10: Margot Petrowski/Dreamstime.com; Zurijeta/iStock/Thinkstock; p. 12: Cynthia Farmer/Dreamstime.com; Digital Vision/Thinkstock; Apostolosmastoris/Dreamstime.com; p. 14: Jupiterimages/Getty Images/Thinkstock; Blend Images/Thinkstock; Ilka-Erika Szasz-Fabian/iStock/Thinkstock; Cynthia Farmer/Dreamstime.com; p. 18: Konstanttin/Dreamstime.com; Melpomenem/iStock/Thinkstock; Photos.com/Thinkstock; p. 19: MrJPEG/iStock/Thinkstock; Sergey Ilin/iStock/Thinkstock; iStock/Thinkstock; Christophe Testi/iStock/Thinkstock; Olga Ryabtsova/iStock/Thinkstock; Mikko PitkSnen/Hemera/Thinkstock; Nikojolle/Dreamstime.com; AGorohov/iStock/Thinkstock; p. 21: Cookelma/iStock/Thinkstock; p. 29: Monkey Business Images/iStock/Thinkstock; Shelly Perry/iStock/Thinkstock; Cathy Yeulet/Hemera/Thinkstock; Monkey Business Images/iStock/Thinkstock; p. 36: Ingram Publishing/Thinkstock; p. 37: Michael Ludwig/Dreamstime.com; Lightpoet/Dreamstime.com; Smon123/Dreamstime.com; Heike Brauer/Hemera/Thinkstock; Tiinasfoto/Dreamstime.com; p. 41: BananaStock/Thinkstock; p. 42: Todd Warnock/Photodisc/Thinkstock; Fuse/Thinkstock; Chris Clinton/Photodisc/Thinkstock; Veronicagomepola/iStock/Thinkstock; Wavebreak Media Ltd./Thinkstock; p. 46: Watcha/iStock/Thinkstock; Nataliya Kuznetsova/iStock/Thinkstock; Topaz777/iStock/Thinkstock; Jozsef Szasz-Fabian/iStock/Thinkstock; Konstantin Tavrov/Hemera/Thinkstock; John Anderson/iStock/Thinkstock; p. 54: Top Photo Corporation Group/Thinkstock; p. 57: Jupiterimages/Liquidlibrary/Thinkstock; Martine De Graaf/Dreamstime.com; Monkey Business Images/iStock/Thinkstock; SanneBerg/iStock/Thinkstock; Sergio Ranalli/Pulsar Imagens (Menino pintado para o Jawari na Aldeia Aiha - Etnia Kalapalo - Parque Indígena do Xingu Local: Querência - MT Data: 07/2011 Tombo: 03SR622); p. 64: Icefront/iStock/Thinkstock; Olvas/iStock/Thinkstock; Darya Petrenko/Dreamstime.com; p. 66: Roman_sh/iStock/Thinkstock; Rafaela Delli Paoli/Alamy/Glowimages; Tiramisu Art Studio/iStock/Thinkstock; p. 67: Chen Ping-hung/Hemera/Thinkstock; Joe Gough/iStock/Thinkstock; Oxana Denezhkina/iStock/Thinkstock; Aida Ricciardiello Caballero/iStock/Thinkstock; Branislav Senic/Dreamstime.com; Barbara Dudzinska/iStock/Thinkstock; p. 74: Moodboard/Thinkstock; Rozenn Leard/Dreamstime.com; Csaba Peterdi/iStock/Thinkstock; BananaStock/Thinkstock; Timmary/iStock/Thinkstock; Kontur-vid/Dreamstime.com; Ryan McVay/Photodisc/Thinkstock; Igor Terekhov/Dreamstime.com; Howard Shooter/Dorling Kindersley/Thinkstock; p. 75: Ingram Publishing/Thinkstock; Martine Doucet/E+/Getty Images; Artranq/iStock/Thinkstock; Greeneinav/Dreamstime.com; Pro777/Dreamstime.com; p. 78: Magone/iStock/Thinkstock; Purestock/Thinkstock; Roman_sh/iStock/Thinkstock; Barbara Dudzinska/iStock/Thinkstock; Ruth Black/iStock/Thinkstock; Digital Vision/Thinkstock; Handmade Pictures/iStock/Thinkstock; Violleta/iStock/Thinkstock; p. 84: Sonya Etchison/Dreamstime.com; Goodshoot/Thinkstock; Image Source/Getty Images; Darryl Estrine/DAJ/Getty Images; p. 85: Fuse/Thinkstock; Fuse/Thinkstock; p. 87: iStock/Thinkstock; Tomas Pavlasek/iStock/Thinkstock; Vladimir Blinov/Dreamstime.com; Tnehala/iStock/Thinkstock; p. 91: Monkey Business Images/Thinkstock; Jupiterimages/Creatas/Thinkstock; George Doyle/Stockbyte/Thinkstock; Photodisc/Thinkstock; Comstock/Stockbyte/Thinkstock; p. 96: Zimindmitry/iStock/Thinkstock; Bezmaski/iStock/Thinkstock; PhotoObjects.ne/Thinkstock; Julißn Rovagnat/Hemera/Thinkstock; Robert Byron/Hemera/Thinkstock; p. 97: Constantin Opris/Dreamstime.com; Mlan61/ Dreamstime.com; Vasiliy Vishnevskiy/Dreamstime.com; Ahara/Dreamstime.com; p. 101: Monkey Business Images/Dreamstime.com; p. 102: Ahmad Ghazali Ahmad Tajuddin/Dreamstime.com; Dmitry Panchenko/Dreamstime.com; Vadim Yerofeyev/Dreamstime.com; Monika Adamczyk/Dreamstime.com; Glenda Powers/Dreamstime.com; p. 107: Valentyn75/Dreamstime.com; Mircea Costina/Dreamstime.com; Nevodka/Dreamstime.com; Image Source White/Thinkstock; p. 109: Stockbyte/Thinkstock; Dimitri Surkov/Dreamstime.com; Finist4/Dreamstime.com; Ana Abrao/Hemera/Thinkstock; Sergiy Zavgorodny/Dreamstime.com; p. 112: Tatniz/iStock/Thinkstock; Evgenyatamanenko/Dreamstime.com; Karin Hildebrand Lau/Dreamstime.com; Marlee/Dreamstime.com; Alesikka/Dreamstime.com; p. 125: Ruth Black/iStock/Thinkstock; Azurita/iStock/Thinkstock; Izabela Wojcicki/iStock/Thinkstock; p. 127: Matt Jeacock/iStock/Thinkstock; AnjelaGr/iStock/Thinkstock; Irina Drazowa-Fischer/iStock/Thinkstock; Photostouch/Dreamstime.com; Brebca/Dreamstime.com; Olga Kriger/Dreamstime.com.

Todos os esforços foram feitos no sentido de encontrar os detentores dos direitos das obras protegidas por copyright. Caso tenha havido alguma omissão involuntária, a editora terá o maior prazer em corrigi-la na primeira oportunidade.

CONTENTS

	WELCOME	4
1	A TALENT SHOW	8
2	AT SCHOOL	16
	REVIEW UNITS 1 - 2	24
3	A SPECIAL PRESENT	26
4	A NICE BOY	34
	REVIEW UNITS 3 - 4	42
5	A BIG CAT	44
6	I'M SORRY!	52
	REVIEW UNITS 5 - 6	60
7	I'M HUNGRY!	62
8	I LIKE SWIMMING.	70
	REVIEW UNITS 7 - 8	78
	GOODBYE	80
	WORKBOOK	81
	INSTRUCTIONS	113
	PROJECT	114
	GLOSSARY	116
	STICKERS	121
	CUTOUTS	129

2 LISTEN, SAY, AND COLOR.

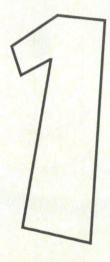
ONE

TWO

THREE

3 LOOK, COUNT, AND CHECK (✓).

A APPLE

B BANANA

C SANDWICH

○ 2 – TWO
○ 3 – THREE

○ 1 – ONE
○ 3 – THREE

○ 1 – ONE
○ 2 – TWO

6 SIX

4 LISTEN, SAY, AND ACT OUT.

5 LISTEN AND SING.

HELLO SAMBA

HELLO, HOW ARE YOU?
HI, I'M OK!
HELLO, HOW ARE YOU?
I'M FINE, THANK YOU. AND YOU?
GOODBYE, GOODBYE, MY FRIEND.
GOODBYE, SEE YOU AGAIN.
GOODBYE, GOODBYE, BYE, BYE!
GOODBYE, SEE YOU, **BYE, BYE!**

1 A TALENT SHOW

1 LOOK, LISTEN, AND ACT OUT.

1 (ONE), 2 (TWO)
1 (ONE), 2 (TWO), 3 (THREE)
1 (ONE), 2 (TWO), 3 (THREE)

PLAY WITH ME!

3 (THREE), 4 (FOUR)
3 (THREE), 4 (FOUR), 5 (FIVE)
3 (THREE), 4 (FOUR), 5 (FIVE)

ONE MORE TIME!

8 EIGHT

3 LISTEN, CHECK (✓), AND ACT OUT.

 HI. I'M MEI. I'M A GIRL.

HELLO. I'M WILL. I'M A BOY.

A

HI. I'M JENNY. I'M A GIRL. ○  HI. I'M THOMAS. I'M A BOY. ○

B

HI. I'M KATY. I'M A GIRL. ○  HI. I'M ROBERT. I'M A BOY. ○

4 LOOK, COUNT, AND WRITE.

 BOYS   GIRLS

5 LISTEN, SAY, AND NUMBER.

| 1 TEACHER | 2 CLASSROOM | 3 SCHOOL |

12 TWELVE

6 LISTEN AND ACT OUT.

7 DRAW.

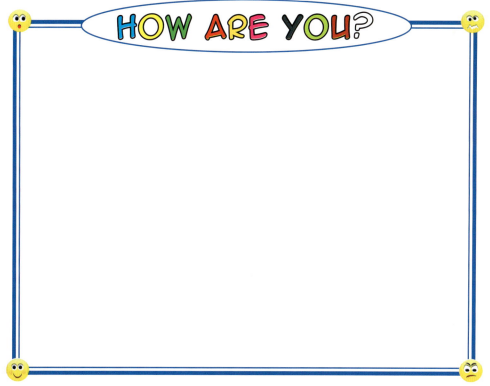

8 **LISTEN AND SING.**

HOW ARE YOU?

DEAR TEACHER, DEAR TEACHER,
HOW ARE YOU? HOW ARE YOU?
I'M FINE, THANK YOU. I'M FINE, THANK YOU!
AND YOU? AND YOU?

9 **LOOK, LISTEN, AND CIRCLE.**

A

B

 TIME TO PLAY

GET THERE!

FIFTEEN

3   LOOK AND CHECK (✓).

4   LISTEN AND NUMBER.

5 LISTEN AND CHECK (✓).

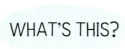 WHAT'S THIS?

A IT'S ○ A PEN  ○ A NOTEBOOK

B IT'S  ○ A BOOK  ○ A PENCIL CASE

C IT'S ○ A PEN ○ AN ERASER

D IT'S ○ A PENCIL SHARPENER  ○ A PENCIL

E IT'S  ○ A SCHOOLBAG  ○ A BOOK

F IT'S ○ AN ERASER  ○ A PENCIL

G IT'S  ○ A NOTEBOOK  ○ A PENCIL CASE

H IT'S ○ A PENCIL SHARPENER  ○ A PEN

6 LISTEN, SAY, AND ACT OUT.

A
RAISE YOUR HAND.

B
OPEN YOUR BOOK.

C
CLOSE YOUR BOOK.

D
BE QUIET, PLEASE.

E
PAY ATTENTION.

F
SIT DOWN.

7 LOOK AND CIRCLE.

PAY ATTENTION.

OPEN YOUR BOOK.

RAISE YOUR HAND.

SIT DOWN.

BE QUIET, PLEASE.

CLOSE YOUR BOOK.

8 LOOK, LISTEN, AND SAY.

6 – SIX   7 – SEVEN   8 – EIGHT   9 – NINE   10 – TEN

9 LOOK AND STICK.

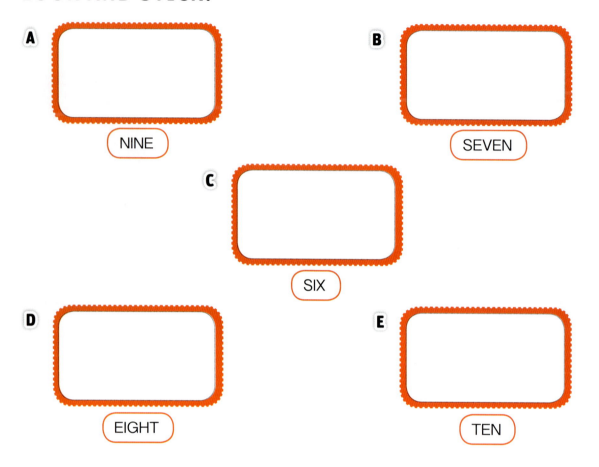

A NINE
B SEVEN
C SIX
D EIGHT
E TEN

10 LOOK, COUNT, AND WRITE.

○ BOOKS   ○ ERASERS   ○ NOTEBOOKS   ○ PENS

○ PENCIL SHARPENERS   ○ PENCILS   ○ PENCIL CASE

22 TWENTY-TWO

11 SING AND COLOR.

LET'S COUNT!

ONE, TWO, THREE, FOUR, FIVE, SIX.

I WANT TO COUNT,

I WANT TO DO LIKE THIS.

SEVEN AND EIGHT, NINE AND TEN.

I WANT TO COUNT

AND DO IT AGAIN!

1, 2, 3 (CLAP), 4, 5, 6 (CLAP),

7 AND 8 (CLAP), 9, AND 10 (CLAP) (2X)

TWENTY-THREE

REVIEW UNITS 1-2

1 LOOK AND CHECK.

TIM: HI, JANE.
JANE: HELLO, TIM.
TIM: HOW ARE YOU?
JANE: I'M FINE, THANKS. AND YOU?
TIM: I'M FINE TOO.

A

B

2 LOOK AND NUMBER.

1. OPEN YOUR BOOK.
2. RAISE YOUR HAND.
3. BE QUIET, PLEASE.
4. SIT DOWN.

3 LISTEN, SAY, AND NUMBER.

4 LOOK, LISTEN, AND MATCH.

HI! I'M JOHNNY. THIS IS MY FAMILY.

HELLO! I'M PATRICIA. THIS IS MY BROTHER.

HI! I'M TOM. THIS IS MY FATHER AND THIS IS MY SISTER.

HELLO! I'M CHRISTINE. THIS IS MY MOTHER.

5 LISTEN AND STICK.

THIS IS MY GRANDFATHER.

THIS IS MY GRANDMOTHER.

THIS IS MY GRANDFATHER.

THIS IS MY GRANDMOTHER.

THIS IS MY FATHER.

THIS IS MY MOTHER.

THIS IS MY SISTER.

I'M VINNY.

6 LISTEN AND SAY.

WHO IS **SHE**?
SHE IS YOKO.

WHO IS **HE**?
HE IS PAUL.

7 LISTEN AND NUMBER.

8 DRAW, SHOW, AND TELL.

I LOVE MY FAMILY.

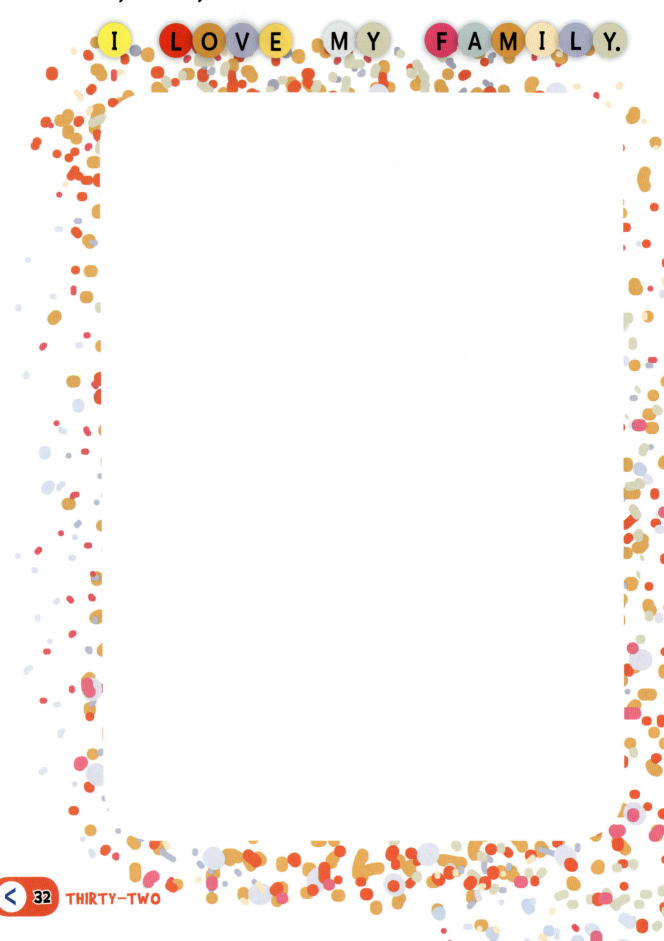

9 CIRCLE, SING, AND COLOR.

THIS IS MY FAMILY!

THIS IS MY FAMILY, FAMILY.

WE LIVE TOGETHER HAPPILY.

THIS IS MY SISTER, THIS IS MY BROTHER,

LITTLE BABY, WE LOVE ONE ANOTHER.

THIS IS MY FAMILY, FAMILY.

WE LIVE TOGETHER HAPPILY.

MY GRANDFATHER, MY GRANDMOTHER,

MOM AND DAD, WE LOVE ONE ANOTHER.

I LOVE MY FAMILY!

TIME TO PLAY

S _ S T E _

4 A NICE BOY

1 LOOK, LISTEN, AND ACT OUT.

3 **LOOK AND COLOR.**

I LOVE MY TOYS!

YELLOW BALL

GREEN CAR

BROWN BIKE

RED SKATEBOARD

BLUE TEDDY BEAR

4 LISTEN AND NUMBER.

THIS IS A YELLOW BALL.

THIS IS A BLUE SKATEBOARD.

THIS IS A RED TEDDY BEAR.

THIS IS A BROWN CAR.

THIS IS A GREEN BIKE.

5 LISTEN, SAY, AND ACT OUT.

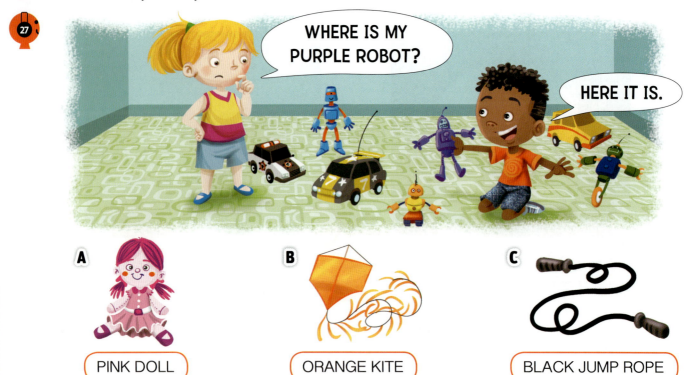

A PINK DOLL
B ORANGE KITE
C BLACK JUMP ROPE

6 LISTEN AND STICK.

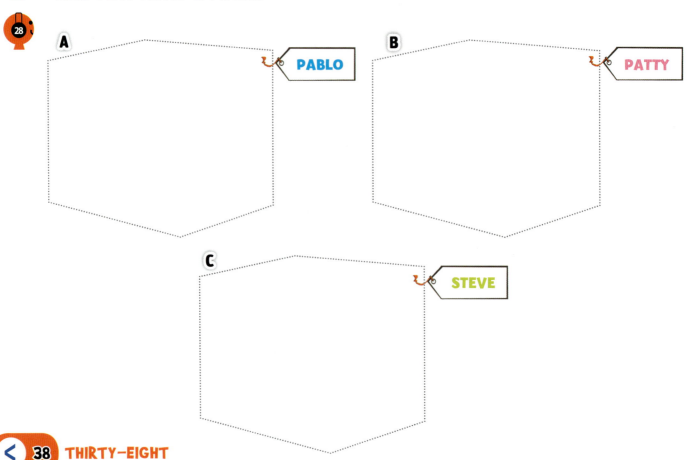

A PABLO
B PATTY
C STEVE

7 LISTEN AND COLOR.

COLORED BALLOONS IN THE AIR

BLUE BALLOONS, RED BALLOONS, WHERE?

PINK BALLOONS, GREEN BALLOONS, THERE!

PURPLE BALLOONS, YELLOW BALLOONS, WHERE?

COLORED BALLOONS IN THE AIR!

BLACK AND BROWN, ORANGE TOO,

COLORED BALLOONS, MY FAVORITE COLOR IS BLUE!

8   LISTEN, POINT, AND ACT OUT.

A: WHAT'S THIS?
B: IT'S A CAR.

A: WHAT COLOR IS IT?
B: IT'S BLACK.

UNITS 3-4

1 LOOK AND MATCH.

WHO IS SHE?   WHO IS HE?

 A

 B

 C

 D

 E

SHE IS MY SISTER.   HE IS MY FATHER.   SHE IS MY MOTHER.

SHE IS MY GRANDMOTHER.   HE IS MY GRANDFATHER.

2. CHOOSE, CHECK (✓), AND DRAW.

WHAT'S THIS?
- ○ IT'S A BIKE.
- ○ IT'S A DOLL.
- ○ IT'S A KITE.

WHAT COLOR IS IT?
- ○ IT'S YELLOW AND RED.
- ○ IT'S GREEN AND BLUE.
- ○ IT'S PINK AND ORANGE.

CHECK YOUR PROGRESS

MY PROGRESS IN ENGLISH IS...

AWESOME · VERY GOOD · GOOD

5

A BIG CAT

 1 LOOK, LISTEN, AND ACT OUT.

HI, JANET.

AND THIS IS MY CAT LOU.

3 MATCH. THEN LISTEN AND SAY.

A A BIG CAT

B A SMALL DOG

4 LISTEN, POINT, AND SAY.

FISH

HAMSTER

TURTLE

BIRD

5 LISTEN, NUMBER, AND COLOR.

BIRD: RED AND BLUE
CAT: YELLOW
DOG: BLACK AND BROWN
FISH: PINK AND PURPLE
HAMSTER: ORANGE
TURTLE: GREEN

FORTY-SEVEN

6 LOOK AND STICK.

A

A _____ FISH

B

A _____ BIRD

C

A _____ DOG

D

A _____ CAT

E

A _____ HAMSTER

F

A _____ TURTLE

7 LISTEN AND IDENTIFY. THEN SING.

CAN I HAVE A PET?

CAN I HAVE A BIG PET?

MOM SAID, NO, NO!

CAN I HAVE A SMALL PET?

MOM SAID, YES, YES!

CAT, DOG, TURTLE, BIRD, FISH, HAMSTER. (2X)

CAT, CAT... MEOW!

DOG, DOG... WOOF!

BIRD, BIRD... TWEET!

HAMSTER... SQUEAK!

8 LOOK, COUNT, AND CHECK (✓).

HOW MANY...?

- A ○ 4 HAMSTERS ○ 3 HAMSTERS
- B ○ 2 CATS ○ 3 CATS
- C ○ 4 DOGS ○ 5 DOGS
- D ○ 3 TURTLES ○ 2 TURTLES
- E ○ 5 BIRDS ○ 6 BIRDS
- F ○ 6 FISH ○ 4 FISH

ANIMAL GAME

3 LOOK AND CIRCLE.

A TINA AND SOPHIE ARE...

TEACHERS.   SISTERS.

B TINA AND SOPHIE HAVE...

BIKES.   SKATEBOARDS.

4 LISTEN, POINT, AND SAY.

1. HEAD
2. ARM
3. HAND
4. LEG
5. FOOT

5   LISTEN, SING, AND ACT OUT.

MOVE... STOP!

CAN YOU MOVE YOUR **HEAD**? (2X)
CAN YOU MOVE YOUR **HEAD**? – STOP!

CAN YOU SHAKE YOUR **HAND**? (2X)
CAN YOU SHAKE YOUR **HAND**? – STOP!

CAN YOU MOVE YOUR **ARM**? (2X)
CAN YOU MOVE YOUR **ARM**? – STOP!

CAN YOU SHAKE YOUR **LEG**? (2X)
CAN YOU SHAKE YOUR **LEG**? – STOP!

CAN YOU MOVE YOUR **FOOT**? (RIGHT FOOT!)
CAN YOU MOVE YOUR **FOOT**? (LEFT FOOT!)
CAN YOU MOVE YOUR **FOOT**? – STOP!

6 DRAW, COLOR, AND STICK.

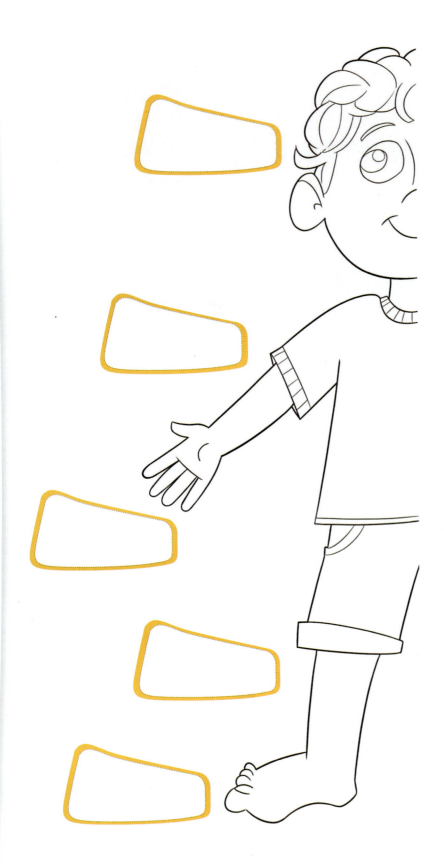

56 FIFTY-SIX

7 LISTEN, FIND, AND SAY.

    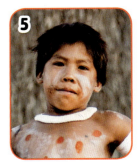

  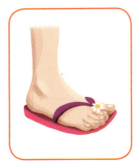  

8 **DRAW YOUR CLASSMATE'S HAND.**

SPOT THE 7 DIFFERENCES

REVIEW UNITS 5-6

1 LOOK AND COLOR.

● ARM   ● FOOT   ● HAND   ● HEAD   ● LEG

2 CIRCLE THE ODD ONE OUT.

FOOT   DOG   ARM   HEAD

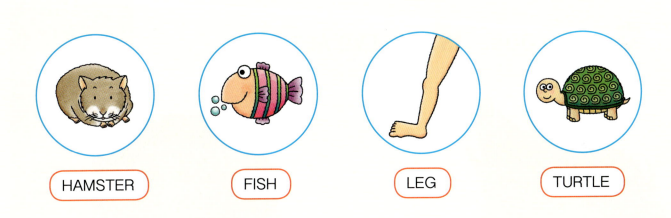

HAMSTER   FISH   LEG   TURTLE

CHECK YOUR PROGRESS

MY PROGRESS IN ENGLISH IS...

AWESOME   VERY GOOD   GOOD

3 LOOK AND MATCH.

A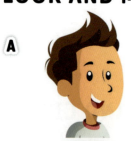

B

C

D

WELL, I DON'T LIKE FRUIT. I LIKE BREAD AND JAM.

AND I LOVE GRAPES!

I'M HUNGRY!

YUMMY... I LOVE APPLES!

4 LISTEN, SAY, AND NUMBER.

1. I DON'T LIKE JAM.   2. I LIKE BREAD.   3. I LOVE JUICE.

5 LOOK, LISTEN, AND STICK.

A
CUPCAKES

B
JUICE

C
FRUIT

D
COOKIES

E
BREAD

F
APPLES

G
MILK

H
GRAPES

I
JAM

6 LISTEN AND SAY. THEN ACT OUT.

FRENCH FRIES

RICE AND BEANS

SOUP

SPAGHETTI

CHICKEN

SALAD

MOTHER:	DO YOU WANT SPAGHETTI, KIDS?
GIRL:	YES, PLEASE. I LOVE SPAGHETTI.
BOY:	NO, THANKS. I DON'T LIKE SPAGHETTI. I LIKE CHICKEN AND SALAD.

7 LOOK AND CHECK (✓).

1. CHICKEN
2. FRENCH FRIES
3. RICE AND BEANS
4. SALAD
5. SOUP
6. SPAGHETTI

A
✓ 2   ◯ 4

B
◯ 3   ◯ 5

C
◯ 1   ◯ 6

D
◯ 3   ◯ 2

E
◯ 1   ◯ 2

F
◯ 6   ◯ 4

8 SING AND COLOR.

I LOVE APPLES!

WHAT DO YOU HAVE FOR BREAKFAST, FOR BREAKFAST?

I HAVE BREAD AND JAM, A GLASS OF JUICE OR A GLASS OF MILK.

(AND I LOVE APPLES, I LOVE APPLES!)

(A GLASS OF MILK, A GLASS OF MILK)

WHAT DO YOU HAVE FOR LUNCH, FOR LUNCH?

I HAVE RICE AND BEANS, FRENCH FRIES, CHICKEN AND SALAD.

(AND I LOVE APPLES, I LOVE APPLES!)

(CHICKEN AND SALAD, CHICKEN AND SALAD)

WHAT DO YOU EAT IN THE AFTERNOON, IN THE AFTERNOON?

COOKIES AND CUPCAKES OR GRAPES.

(AND I LOVE APPLES, I LOVE APPLES!)

(OR GRAPES, OR GRAPES)

WHAT DO YOU HAVE FOR DINNER, FOR DINNER?

SOUP OR SPAGHETTI,

SPAGHETTI OR SOUP.

(AND I LOVE APPLES, I LOVE APPLES!)

(SPAGHETTI OR SOUP, SPAGHETTI OR SOUP)

MY MOM ALWAYS SAYS – AN APPLE A, DAY KEEPS THE DOCTOR AWAY!

(AND I LOVE APPLES, I LOVE APPLES!)

(AWAY, AWAY)

(KEEPS THE DOCTOR AWAY!) (2X)

AWAY!

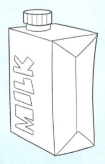
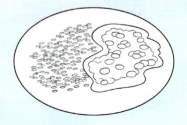

TIME TO PLAY

MEMORY CHAIN GAME

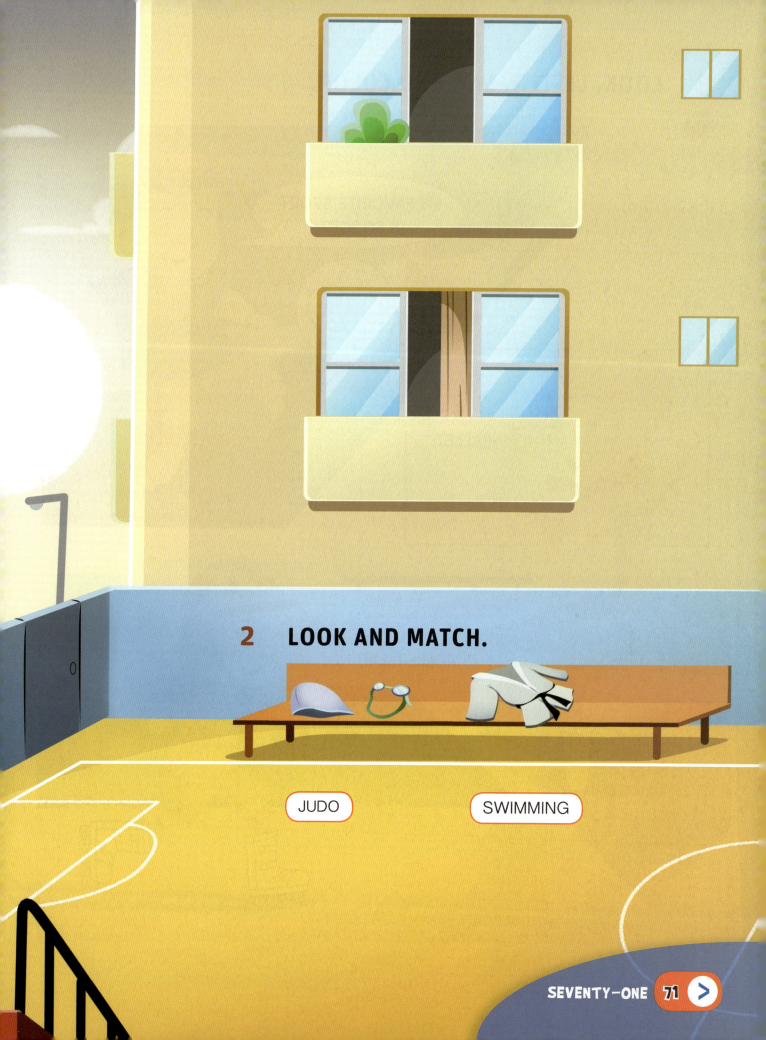

2 LOOK AND MATCH.

JUDO   SWIMMING

3 LOOK, LISTEN, SAY, AND COLOR.

4 HELP WILL FIND HIS FAVORITE SPORT.

5 LISTEN AND CIRCLE.

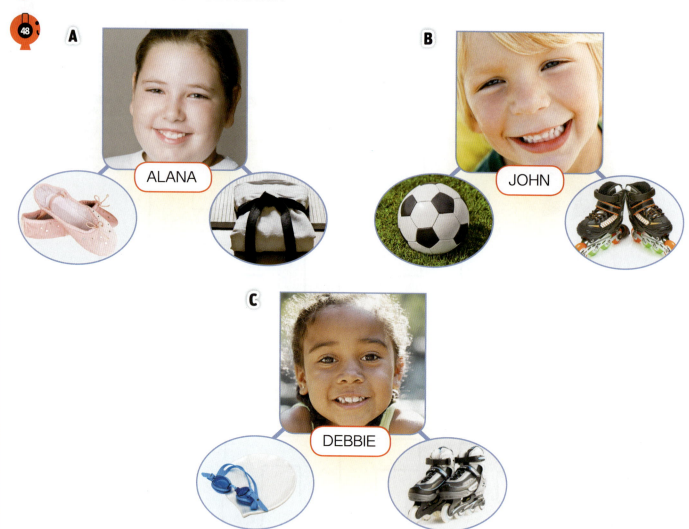

6 DRAW AND COLOR.

WHAT'S YOUR FAVORITE SPORT?

7 LISTEN AND STICK.

SEVENTY-FIVE 75

8 LISTEN, CIRCLE, AND SING.

WHAT'S YOUR FAVORITE SPORT?

PLAY, DO, GO, AND DANCE. (2X)

WHAT DO YOU PLAY?

I PLAY SOCCER!

WHAT DO YOU DO?

I DO JUDO!

PLAY, DO, GO, AND DANCE. (2X)

WHAT DO YOU DANCE?

I'M A BALLET DANCER!

HOW ABOUT YOU?

I GO ROLLERBLADING!

PLAY, DO, GO, AND DANCE.

WHAT'S YOUR FAVORITE SPORT? (2X)

SPORTS GAME

THE WINNER!

START

REVIEW UNITS 7-8

1 LOOK AND CHECK (✓).

A
A: DO YOU WANT SPAGHETTI?
B: YES, PLEASE.

B
A: DO YOU LIKE SALAD?
B: YES, I LOVE SALAD.

C
A: YUMMY! I LOVE JAM!
B: I LOVE JAM TOO.

D
A: WHAT'S YOUR FAVORITE JUICE?
B: I LOVE APPLE JUICE.

2 LOOK AND NUMBER.

1 BALLET   2 JUDO   3 ROLLERBLADING
4 SOCCER   5 SWIMMING

CHECK YOUR PROGRESS

IT'S THE END OF THE YEAR!
MY PROGRESS IN ENGLISH IS...

AWESOME

VERY GOOD

GOOD

| NAME | CLASS | DATE |

1 LOOK, COUNT, AND COLOR.

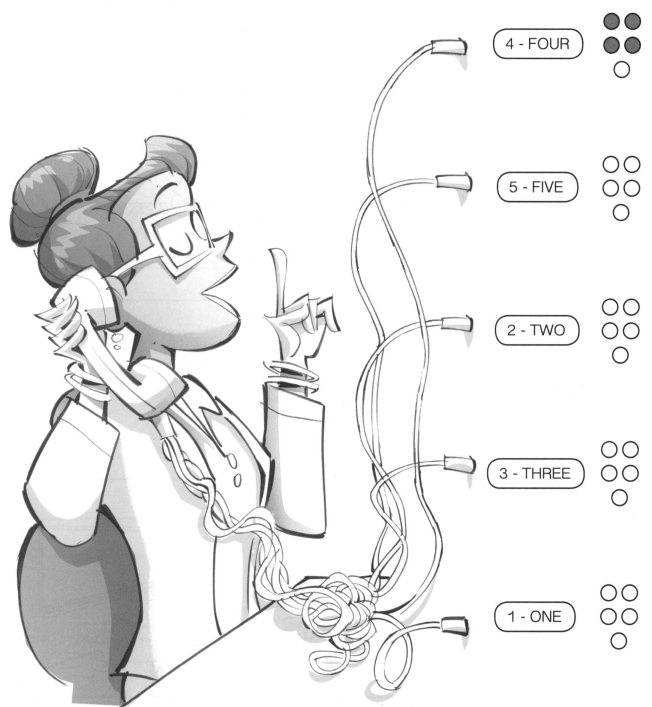

EIGHTY-ONE 81

2 MATCH AND COLOR.

A BOY

B CLASSROOM

C SCHOOL

D TEACHER

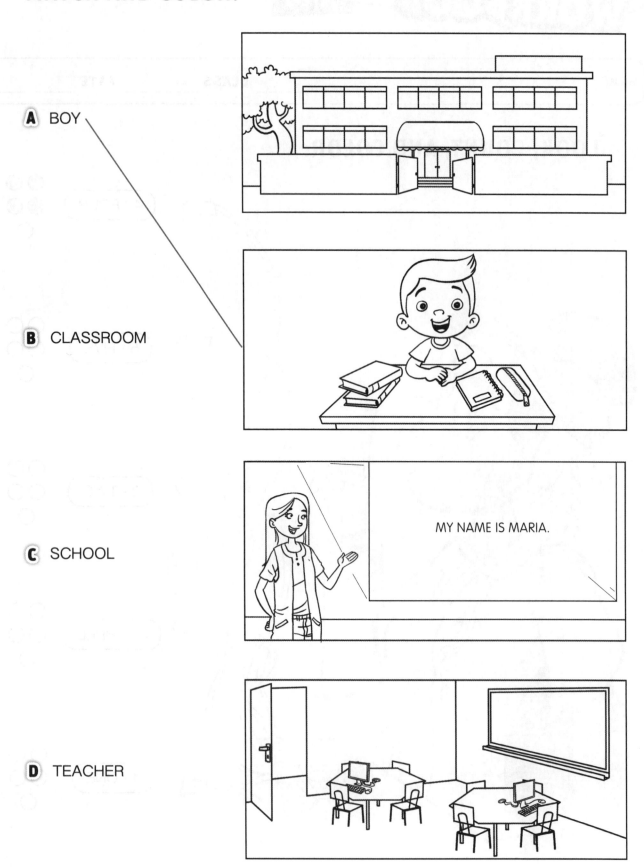

3 CONNECT THE DOTS AND COLOR.

4 DRAW AND COMPLETE.

5 LOOK AND NUMBER.

1
SANDRA: HELLO, I'M SANDRA.
MARIA: HI, SANDRA. I'M MARIA.

2
JANE: HOW ARE YOU?
BARBARA: I'M FINE. AND YOU?
JANE: I'M NOT SO GOOD.

3
ROSS: HELLO, MAX!
MAX: HI, ROSS!

4
PETER: GOODBYE, MOM.
MOM: BYE, PETER.

WORKBOOK — UNIT 2

NAME _____ CLASS _____ DATE _____

1 LOOK AND CIRCLE.

A

BYE!

THANK YOU.

B

SIT DOWN

HELLO!

EIGHTY-FIVE

2 LOOK AND CHECK (✓).

NAOMI	VINNY		
		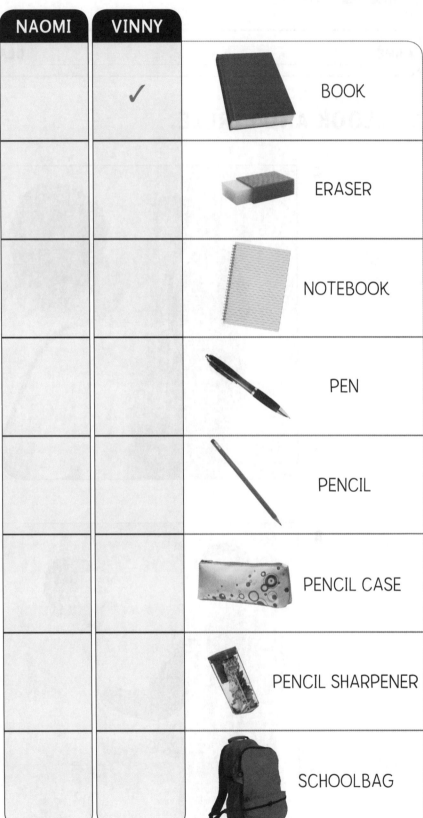	BOOK
	✓		
			ERASER
			NOTEBOOK
			PEN
			PENCIL
			PENCIL CASE
			PENCIL SHARPENER
			SCHOOLBAG

3 ADD, DRAW, AND WRITE.

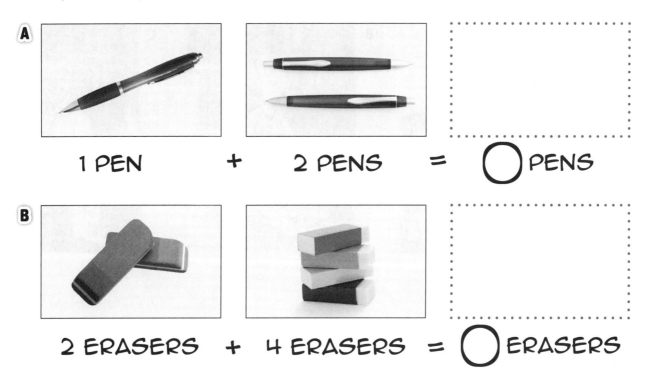

A 1 PEN + 2 PENS = ◯ PENS

B 2 ERASERS + 4 ERASERS = ◯ ERASERS

4 COUNT AND MATCH.

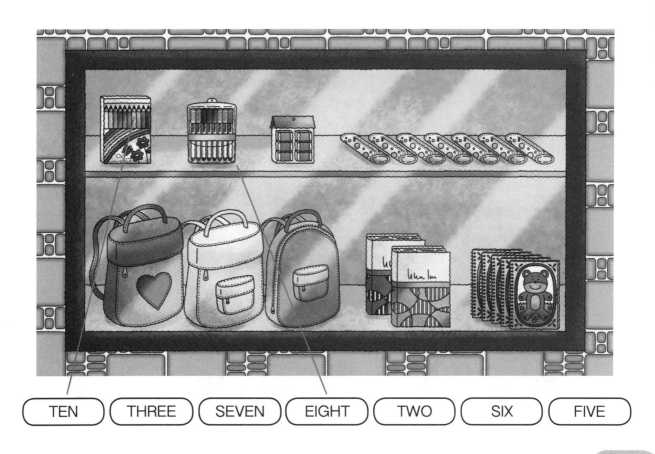

TEN · THREE · SEVEN · EIGHT · TWO · SIX · FIVE

5 LOOK AND MATCH.

A

B

C

(BE QUIET, PLEASE.)   (RAISE YOUR HAND.)   (PAY ATTENTION.)

(OPEN YOUR BOOK.)   (CLOSE YOUR BOOK.)   (SIT DOWN.)

D

E

F

| NAME | CLASS | DATE |

1 HELP WILL FIND HIS...

BROTHER
FATHER
MOTHER
SISTER

EIGHTY-NINE 89

2 FIND AND CIRCLE.

3 LOOK AND CHECK (✓).

HI. I'M KEVIN.

THIS IS MY DAD. ◯
THIS IS MY MOM. ✓

THIS IS MY BROTHER. ◯
THIS IS MY GRANDFATHER. ◯

THIS IS MY BABY BROTHER. ◯
THIS IS MY SISTER. ◯

THIS IS MY GRANDFATHER. ◯
THIS IS MY DAD. ◯

4 LOOK AND NUMBER.

○ A: WHO IS SHE?
　 B: SHE IS MEI.

○ A: WHO IS SHE?
　 B: SHE IS NAOMI.

○ A: WHO IS HE?
　 B: HE IS WILL.

1 A: WHO IS HE?
　 B: HE IS VINNY.

NAME _____ CLASS _____ DATE _____

1   **FIND AND CIRCLE THE BALL.**

NINETY-THREE 93

2 COUNT AND CHECK (✓).

- A ◯ 5 BALLS ◯ 6 BALLS ✓ 4 BALLS
- B ◯ 3 BIKES ◯ 1 BIKE ◯ 2 BIKES
- C ◯ 4 DOLLS ◯ 5 DOLLS ◯ 3 DOLLS
- D ◯ 2 JUMP ROPES ◯ 3 JUMP ROPES ◯ 1 JUMP ROPE

3 **CONNECT THE DOTS AND COLOR. THEN CHECK (✓).**

A IT'S A DOLL. ◯

B IT'S A TEDDY BEAR. ◯

NINETY-FIVE 95

4 MATCH.

THIS IS A KITE.

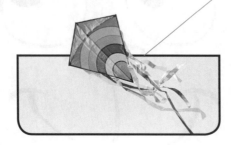

THIS IS A SKATEBOARD.

THIS IS A CAR.

THIS IS A ROBOT.

THIS IS A BIKE.

UNIT 5

| NAME | CLASS | DATE |

1 JOIN THE DOTS AND COLOR.

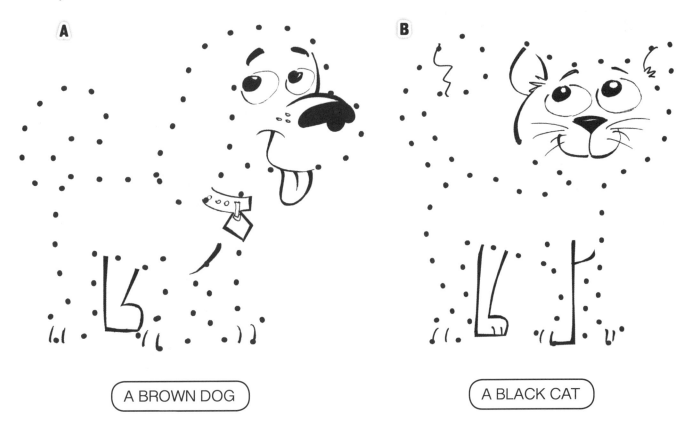

A BROWN DOG

A BLACK CAT

2 LOOK AND CIRCLE.

DOG (FISH)   BIRD CAT   CAT HAMSTER   TURTLE DOG

NINETY-SEVEN

3 MATCH.

A (A BIG FISH)

B (A SMALL HAMSTER)

C (A SMALL CAT)

D (A BIG BIRD)

E (A BIG DOG)

F (A SMALL TURTLE)

4 DRAW AND COLOR.

TWO YELLOW BIRDS

ONE BROWN TURTLE

5 FIND, CIRCLE, AND MATCH.

BIRD   CAT   DOG   FISH   HAMSTER   TURTLE

100 ONE HUNDRED

NAME_____ CLASS_____ DATE_____

1 LOOK AND NUMBER.

1 ARM   **2** LEG   **3** HEAD   **4** FOOT   **5** HAND

ONE HUNDRED ONE 101

2 FIND, CIRCLE, AND MATCH.

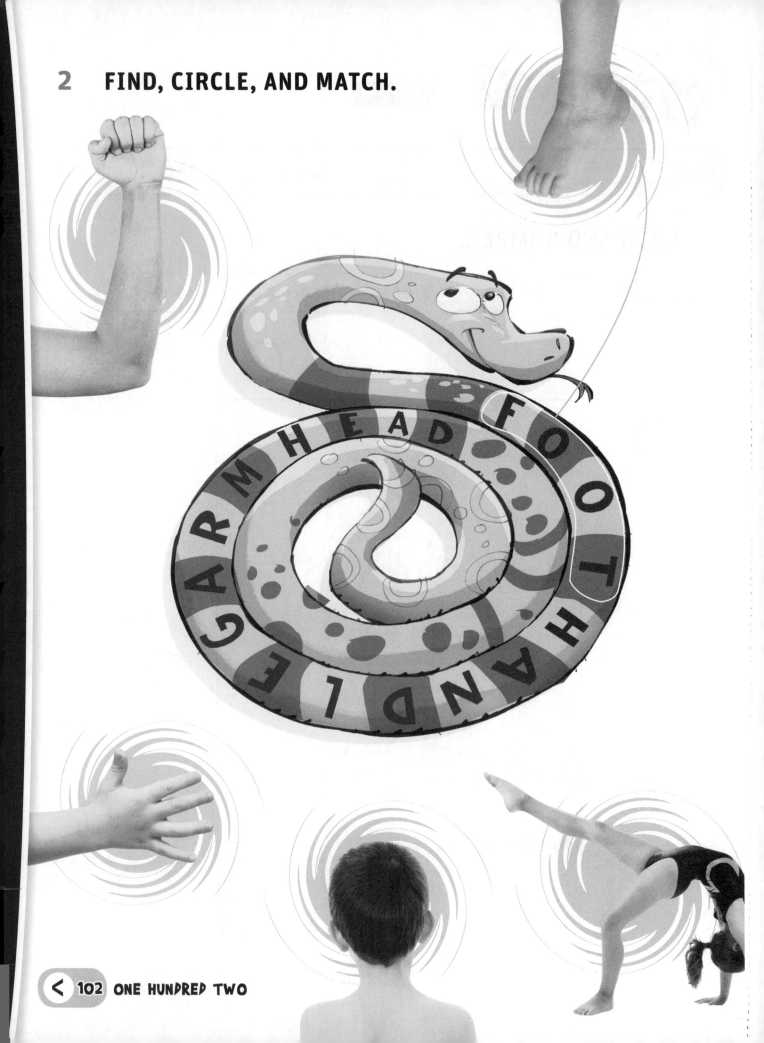

3 DRAW, CHECK (✓), AND COLOR.

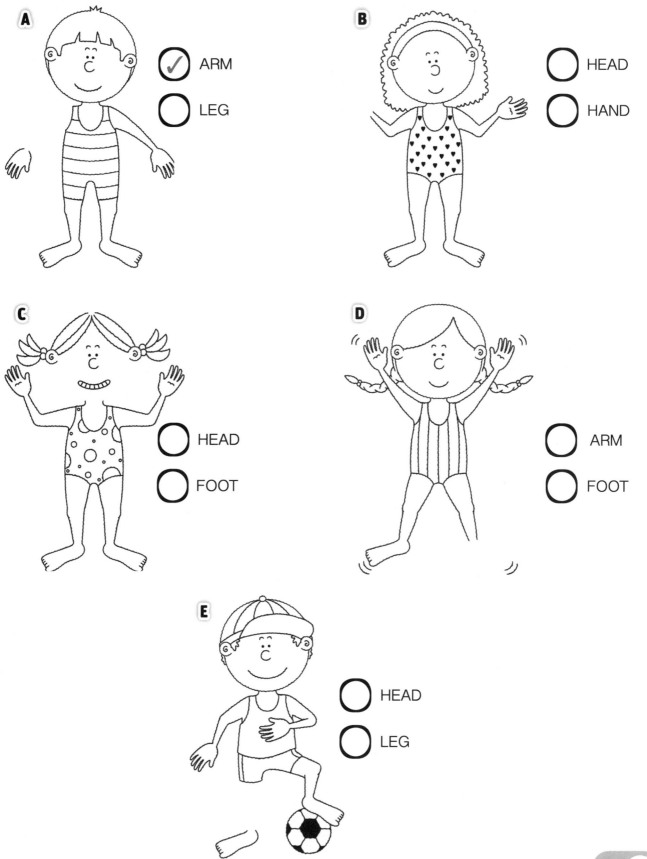

4 LOOK AND CIRCLE.

NAME _____ CLASS _____ DATE _____

1 LOOK AND CHECK (✓).

	BREAD AND JAM	CHICKEN	FRENCH FRIES	JUICE	MILK	RICE AND BEANS	SALAD	SPAGHETTI
ADAM				✓				
EMMA								
JAKE								

2 LOOK, MATCH, AND DRAW.

I LIKE...   I DON'T LIKE...   I LOVE...

A

(I LIKE GRAPES.)

B

(I LOVE JAM.)

C

(I DON'T LIKE FRENCH FRIES.)

D

(I LOVE ORANGE JUICE.)

3 LOOK AND CIRCLE.

DO YOU WANT...?

4 CHECK (✓) AND DRAW.

I LIKE...

- ◯ APPLES
- ◯ COOKIES
- ◯ GRAPES
- ◯ RICE

- ◯ BEANS
- ◯ CUPCAKES
- ◯ JAM
- ◯ SALAD

- ◯ BREAD
- ◯ FRENCH FRIES
- ◯ JUICE
- ◯ SOUP

- ◯ CHICKEN
- ◯ FRUIT
- ◯ MILK
- ◯ SPAGHETTI

WORKBOOK — UNIT 8

NAME _____ CLASS _____ DATE _____

1 LOOK AND CHECK (✓).

A
- ○ BALLET
- ○ ROLLERBLADING

B
- ✓ SOCCER
- ○ SWIMMING

C
- ○ SOCCER
- ○ JUDO

D
- ○ JUDO
- ○ ROLLERBLADING

E
- ○ SWIMMING
- ○ BALLET

ONE HUNDRED NINE 109

2 LOOK AND MATCH.

A SWIMMING

B ROLLERBLADING

C SOCCER

D BALLET

E JUDO

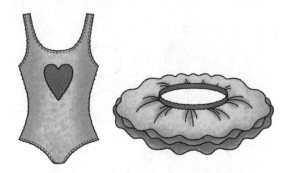

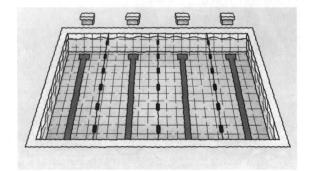

3 LOOK AND NUMBER.

1 HI. I'M TINA. I LIKE SWIMMING.

2 HI. I'M PRISCILA. MY FAVORITE SPORT IS ROLLERBLADING.

3 HELLO. MY NAME IS EDWARD. I LOVE JUDO!

4 LOOK AND COLOR.

DO YOU LIKE...?

A
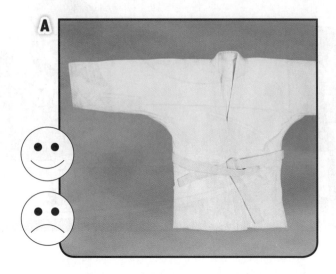

B
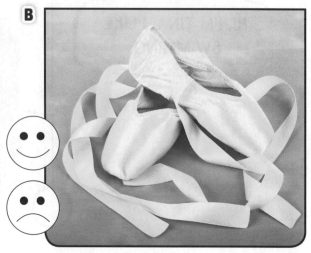

C
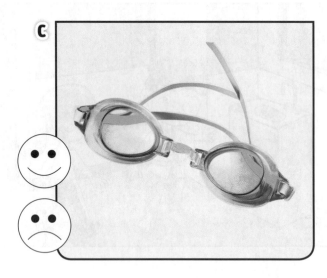

D

E
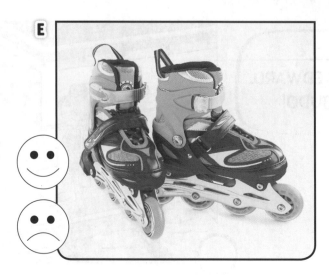

ACT OUT: ENCENE

ADD: SOME

CHECK: ASSINALE

CHOOSE: ESCOLHA

CIRCLE: CIRCULE

CLAP: BATA PALMAS

COLOR: PINTE

COMPLETE: COMPLETE

COUNT: CONTE

DRAW: DESENHE

FIND: ENCONTRE

FIND OUT: DESCUBRA

HELP: AJUDE

IDENTIFY: IDENTIFIQUE

CONNECT THE DOTS: LIGUE OS PONTOS

LISTEN: ESCUTE

LOOK: OBSERVE

MATCH: LIGUE

NUMBER: NUMERE

POINT: APONTE

SAY: DIGA

SHOW AND TELL: MOSTRE E APRESENTE

SING: CANTE

STICK: COLE

WRITE: ESCREVA

PROJECT
DONATION IS LOVE!

1 LOOK AND SAY: WHAT ARE NAOMI AND WILL DOING?

2 LOOK AND CIRCLE.

CAR   DOLL   ROBOT   SKATEBOARD   TEDDY BEAR

3 DRAW.

MY TOYS FOR DONATION.

GLOSSARY

A

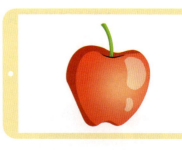

APPLE: MAÇÃ
ARM: BRAÇO

B

BALL: BOLA
BALLET: BALÉ

BANANA: BANANA
BEANS: FEIJÃO
BIG: GRANDE
BIKE: BICICLETA

BIRD: PÁSSARO
BLACK: PRETO(A)
BLUE: AZUL
BOOK: LIVRO

BOY: MENINO
BREAD: PÃO
BROTHER: IRMÃO
BROWN: MARROM
BYE: TCHAU

C

- **CAR:** CARRO
- **CAT:** GATO
- **CHICKEN:** FRANGO
- **CLASSMATE:** COLEGA DE TURMA
- **CLASSROOM:** SALA DE AULA
- **COOKIE:** BISCOITO
- **CUPCAKE:** BOLO PEQUENO, ASSADO EM FORMINHA SEMELHANTE A UMA XÍCARA

D

- **DOG:** CACHORRO
- **DOLL:** BONECA

E

- **EIGHT:** OITO
- **ERASER:** BORRACHA

F

- **FAMILY:** FAMÍLIA
- **FATHER:** PAI
- **FISH:** PEIXE
- **FIVE:** CINCO
- **FOOT:** PÉ
- **FOUR:** QUATRO
- **FRENCH FRIES:** BATATA FRITA
- **FRUIT:** FRUTA(S)

G

GIRL: MENINA
GOODBYE: TCHAU
GRANDFATHER: AVÔ
GRANDMOTHER: AVÓ
GRAPE: UVA
GREEN: VERDE

H

HAMSTER: HAMSTER
HAND: MÃO
HEAD: CABEÇA
HUNGRY: FAMINTO(A)

J

JAM: GELEIA
JUDO: JUDÔ
JUICE: SUCO
JUMP ROPE: CORDA DE PULAR

K

KITE: PIPA, PAPAGAIO, PANDORGA

L

LEG: PERNA
LIKE: GOSTAR
LOVE: ADORAR; AMAR

M

MILK: LEITE

MOTHER: MÃE

N

NINE: NOVE

NOTEBOOK: CADERNO

O

ONE: UM

ORANGE: LARANJA

P

PEN: CANETA

PENCIL: LÁPIS

PENCIL CASE: ESTOJO

PENCIL SHARPENER: APONTADOR

PINK: ROSA

PURPLE: ROXO(A)

R

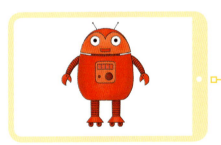

RED: VERMELHO(A)

RICE: ARROZ

ROBOT: ROBÔ

ROLLERBLADING: PATINAÇÃO

S

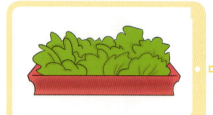

SALAD: SALADA
SANDWICH: SANDUÍCHE
SCHOOL: ESCOLA
SCHOOLBAG: MOCHILA
SEVEN: SETE
SISTER: IRMÃ
SIX: SEIS
SKATEBOARD: *SKATE*
SMALL: PEQUENO(A)
SOCCER: FUTEBOL
SOUP: SOPA
SPAGHETTI: ESPAGUETE
SPORT: ESPORTE
SWIMMING: NATAÇÃO

T

TEACHER: PROFESSOR(A)
TEDDY BEAR: URSINHO DE PELÚCIA
TEN: DEZ
THREE: TRÊS
TURTLE: TARTARUGA
TWO: DOIS

W

WANT: QUERER

Y

YELLOW: AMARELO(A)

UNIT 1

PAGE 9

UNIT 2

PAGE 22

ONE HUNDRED TWENTY-ONE 121

UNIT 3
PAGE 30

UNIT 4
PAGE 38

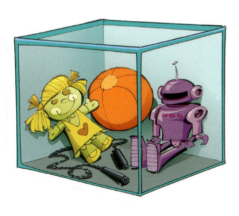 

UNIT 5

PAGE 48

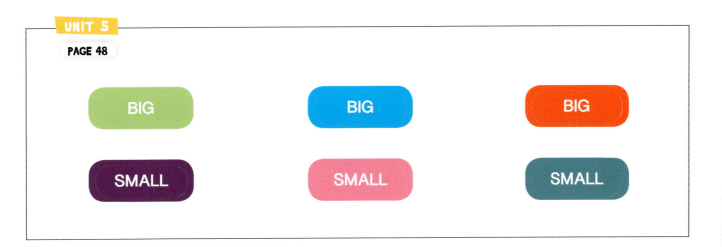

UNIT 6

PAGE 56

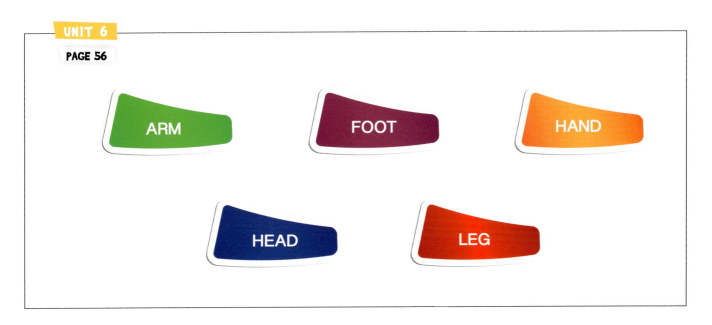

UNIT 7

PAGE 65

ONE HUNDRED TWENTY-FIVE   125

UNIT 7
PAGE 65

UNIT 8
PAGE 75

BALLET   JUDO   ROLLERBLADING

SOCCER   SWIMMING

ONE HUNDRED TWENTY-SEVEN 127

TIME TO PLAY

1	2	3
4	5	6

UNIT 5

THIS IS A _____.

IT IS A _____ DOG.

THIS IS A _____.

IT IS A _____ TURTLE.

THIS IS A _____.

IT IS A _____ HAMSTER.

ONE HUNDRED THIRTY-ONE

UNIT 5

THIS IS A _____.

IT IS A _____ CAT.

THIS IS A _____.

IT IS A _____ FISH.

THIS IS A _____.

IT IS A _____ BIRD.

ONE HUNDRED THIRTY-THREE 133

UNIT 5

YOU TABBIE

TUTORIAL DE ACESSO

Plataforma iOS

1. Acesse a AppStore
2. Digite "You Tabbie" no campo de busca
3. Localize o livro digital e/ou e-Book que deseja baixar
4. Clique na imagem correspondente ao livro
5. Aguarde a instalação e clique em abrir
6. No campo "Login", digite Macmillan
7. Digite a senha que veio no seu livro impresso
8. Navegue pelo seu livro digital

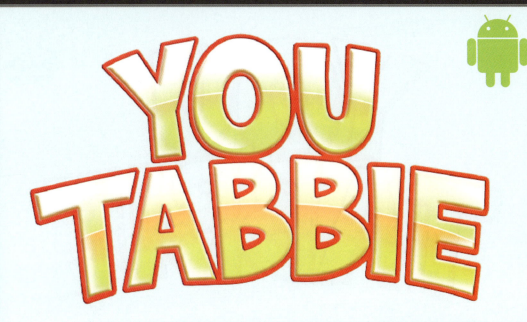

YOU TABBIE

TUTORIAL DE ACESSO

Plataforma ANDROID

1. Acesse a Play Store
2. Digite "You Tabbie" no campo de busca
3. Localize o livro digital e/ou e-Book que deseja baixar
4. Clique na imagem correspondente ao livro
5. Aguarde a instalação e clique em abrir
6. Digite a senha que veio no seu livro impresso
7. Navegue pelo seu livro digital

GUIA PARA OS PAIS

BAIXE OS LIVROS DIGITAIS E OS *E-BOOKS* DE YOUTABBIE E DIVIRTA-SE APRENDENDO INGLÊS COM SEUS FILHOS!

5 LIVROS DIGITAIS INTERATIVOS ESPECIALMENTE DESENVOLVIDOS PARA USAR NO COMPUTADOR E *TABLETS*!

5 *E-BOOKS* QUE RETOMAM VALORES APRESENTADOS AO LONGO DA COLEÇÃO. ÁUDIO, IMAGENS CATIVANTES E MUITA INTERATIVIDADE.

CADA *E-BOOK* TRAZ ATIVIDADES LÚDICAS QUE DESAFIAM SEU FILHO A BUSCAR SOLUÇÕES.

AO LER AS HISTÓRIAS, O ALUNO ACOMPANHA O ÁUDIO EM INGLÊS E PODE OUVIR CADA PALAVRA SEPARADAMENTE.

VIRE A PÁGINA E SAIBA COMO BAIXAR OS COMPONENTES DIGITAIS DE YOUTABBIE.

COMO BAIXAR OS COMPONENTES DIGITAIS

PARA FAZER O *DOWNLOAD* DOS LIVROS DIGITAIS E DOS *E-BOOKS* ENTRE NO SITE:

www.macmillan.com.br/youtabbie

DEPOIS ESCOLHA A PLATAFORMA QUE ESTIVER UTILIZANDO.

CLIQUE NO LIVRO DIGITAL QUE DESEJA BAIXAR. DIGITE A SENHA QUE ESTÁ NO ADESIVO DA TERCEIRA CAPA DO LIVRO IMPRESSO CORRESPONDENTE E AGUARDE A INSTALAÇÃO COMPLETA.

PARA BAIXAR OS *E-BOOKS* CLIQUE NA CAPA E AGUARDE A INSTALAÇÃO. USE A MESMA SENHA.

OS LIVROS DIGITAIS E OS E-BOOKS TAMBÉM ESTÃO DISPONÍVEIS NA APP STORE E GOOGLE PLAY. DIGITE YOUTABBIE E CLIQUE EM *INSTALL*.

DISPONÍVEL PARA:

 Windows XP, Vista, 7 ou 8

 Mac, iPad 2 ou superior

 Dispositivos com Android 2.6 ou superior

www.macmillan.com.br
(11) 4613-2278 / 0800-168877

INTERNAL CODE 9786685724806

FOTOS: DREAMSTIME.COM